Purpose, Meaning, and Passion

HBR EMOTIONAL INTELLIGENCE SERIES

HBR Emotional Intelligence Series

The HBR Emotional Intelligence Series features smart, essential reading on the human side of professional life from the pages of *Harvard Business Review*.

Authentic Leadership

Dealing with Difficult People

Empathy

Happiness

Influence and Persuasion

Leadership Presence

Mindfulness

Purpose, Meaning, and Passion

Resilience

Other books on emotional intelligence from *Harvard Business Review*:

HBR's 10 Must Reads on Emotional Intelligence

HBR Guide to Emotional Intelligence

HBR Everyday Emotional Intelligence

Purpose, Meaning, and Passion

HBR EMOTIONAL INTELLIGENCE SERIES

Harvard Business Review Press

Boston, Massachusetts

10 9 8

Library of Congress Cataloging-in-Publication Data

Title: Purpose, meaning, and passion.
Other titles: HBR emotional intelligence series.
Description: Boston, Massachusetts : Harvard Business Review Press, [2018] | Series: HBR emotional intelligence series
Identifiers: LCCN 2017053590 | ISBN 9781633696273 (pbk. : alk. paper)
Subjects: LCSH: Work--Psychological aspects. | Job satisfaction. | Meaning (Psychology) | Employee motivation. | Enthusiasm.
Classification: LCC BF481 .P87 2018 | DDC 158.7--dc23 LC record available at https://lccn.loc.gov/2017053590

Contents

Contents

Contents

Purpose, Meaning, and Passion

HBR EMOTIONAL INTELLIGENCE SERIES

1

Finding Meaning at Work, Even When Your Job Is Dull

By Morten Hansen and Dacher Keltner

D o you experience meaning at work—or just emptiness?

In the United States, people spend an average of 35 to 40 hours working every week. That's some 80,000 hours during a career—more time than you will spend with your kids probably. Beyond the paycheck, what does work give you? Few questions could be more important. It is sad to walk through life experiencing work as empty, dreadful, a chore—something that saps energy out of your body and soul. Yet many employees feel this way, as evidenced by one large-scale study showing that only 31% of employees were engaged.[1]

Work can, however, provide an array of meaningful experiences, even though many employees do not enjoy them in their current job. So what are the sources of meaningful experiences at work?

We have compiled a list based on our reading of literature in organization behavior and psychology. Many theories speak to meaning at work, including need-based, motivational, status, power, and community theories. The phrase "meaning at work" refers to a person's experience of something meaningful—something of value—that work provides. That is not the same as "meaningful work," which refers to the task itself. Work is a social arena that offers other kinds of meaningful experiences as well.

Before we run through the list, it is important to note:

- Different people look for different types of meaning.

- Different workplaces provide different meanings.

Purpose

Contributions beyond yourself

The people at nonprofit Kiva channel microloans to poor people who can use the money to get a small business going and improve their lives. Their work clearly has a greater purpose—that of helping people in need. This taps into a longing to have a meaningful life defined as making contributions beyond oneself.

The problem is, however, that most work doesn't have such a higher purpose, either because the job is basically mundane or because—let's face it—the company doesn't really have a social mission. Critics of workplace culture like economics researcher Umair Haque argue that work that involves selling yet more burgers, sugar water, high-fashion clothing, and the like has no broader purpose whatsoever. In this view, Coke's "Open happiness" tagline is just a slogan devoid of meaning. However, as researchers Teresa Amabile and Steve Kramer argue, much work can be

5

infused with some level of purpose. (See chapter 9 of this book for more on gradual steps toward meaningful work.) Companies that make real efforts in social responsibilities do this. For example, Danone, the $25 billion large and highly successful consumer goods company that sells yogurt, has defined their business as providing healthy foods (which led them to sell off their biscuit business). The litmus test here is whether employees experience that their work makes positive contributions to others. If they do, then they experience meaning at work.

Self-realization

Learning

Many MBA graduates flock to McKinsey, BCG, and other consultancies so that they can rapidly acquire valuable skills. General Electric is renowned for developing general managers, and people who want to become marketers crave to learn that trade at Procter & Gamble. Work offers opportunities to learn, expand one's horizon, and improve self-awareness. This kind of personal growth is meaningful.

Accomplishment

Work is also a place to accomplish things and be recognized, which leads to greater satisfaction, confidence, and self-worth. In the documentary *Jiro Dreams of Sushi* we see Japan's greatest sushi chef devote his life to making perfect sushi. Some critics like Lucy Kellaway at the *Financial Times* say there isn't a real social mission here. But the main character's quest for perfection—to make better sushi all the time—gives his life a deep sense of meaning. And for Jiro, the work itself—making the sushi—gives him a deep intrinsic satisfaction.

7

Prestige

Status

At cocktail parties, a frequent question is "Where do you work?" The ability to rattle off "Oh, I am a doctor at Harvard Medical School" oozes status. For some, that moment is worth all the grueling night shifts. A high-status organization confers respect, recognition, and a sense of worth to employees, and that provides meaning at work for some.

Power

As Paul Lawrence and Nitin Nohria write about in their book *Driven*, for those drawn to power, work provides an arena for acquiring and exercising power. You may not be one of those, but if you are, you experience work as meaningful because you have and can use power.

Social rewards

Belonging to a community

Companies like Southwest Airlines go out of their way to create a company atmosphere where people feel they belong. In a society where people increasingly are "bowling alone," people crave a place where they can forge friendships and experience a sense of community. (In his book of the same name, Robert Putnam describes the American decline in bowling leagues as a metaphor for a larger cultural shift away from formal social structures.[2]) The workplace can complement or even be a substitute for other communities (family, the neighborhood, clubs and so on). Workplaces that provide a sense of community give people meaning.

Agency

Employees also experience meaning at work when what they do actually matters for the organization, when their ideas are listened to and when they see that their contributions have an impact on how the place performs. A sense of real involvement gives people meaning.

Autonomy

As Dan Pink shows in his book *Drive*, autonomy—the absence of others who tell you what to do and the freedom to do your own work in your own time—is a great intrinsic motivator. Some people are drawn to certain kinds of work that provides a great deal of autonomy. For example, entrepreneurs frequently go into business by themselves so that they can be their own boss. This kind of freedom gives work meaning.

———————————

There are no doubt other sources as well, but the ones listed here seem to be especially important. Which of them are important to you? And which do you receive from your current workplace? Having more sources of meaning is not necessarily better; experiencing one deeply may just be enough. But it's an issue if you don't experience any at all.

MORTEN HANSEN is a professor at the University of California, Berkeley, and at INSEAD, France, and is the author of *Collaboration*: *How Leaders Avoid the Traps, Build Common Ground, and Reap Big Results* (Harvard Business Review Press, 2009). DACHER KELTNER is a professor of psychology at UC Berkeley and the author of *Born to Be Good: The Science of a Meaningful Life* (W. W. Norton, 2009).

Notes

1. "Employee Engagement Research Report," Blessing White, January 2013; http://blessingwhite.com/research-report/ 2013/01/01/employee-engagement-research-report -update-jan-2013.

2. R. D. Putnam, *Bowling Alone: The Collapse and Revival of American Community* (New York: Touchstone Books, 2001).

Adapted from content posted on hbr.org, originally published December 20, 2012 (product #H009WH).

2

What to Do When Your Heart Isn't in Your Work Anymore

By Andy Molinsky

n an ideal world, our work lives would be completely fulfilling, full of meaning, and intrinsically motivating. But what if they're not? What if you're stuck in a job or a career that you once loved, but your heart isn't in it anymore?

More people fit this profile than you'd think. According to a 2017 Gallup survey, only one-third of U.S. employees feel engaged at work; that is, only one in three workers brings a consistently high level of initiative, commitment, passion, and productivity to their job.[1] That leaves the majority of employees less than satisfied with their work.

And truth be told, there could be any number of reasons for this sense of malaise. You might feel stuck doing the same thing over and over again. You might question the ultimate meaning of the work you're doing. You might feel micromanaged or that company leaders don't know or care about your learning and growth. Or maybe your own growth and development since starting your career has caused you to change your passions and priorities in life.

I see and hear examples of career malaise all the time—in my work teaching and training people in companies, in discussions following my corporate talks, and in conversations with my family and friends. Though the tendency among some of us in this situation is to simply grin and bear it, current scientific research suggests ways to reimagine—or reenvision—an uninspired professional existence.

Assess what you want out of your work— at this point in your life

Not everyone wants a high-powered career. In fact, according to research by Yale associate professor of organizational psychology Amy Wrzesniewski, people tend to fall into one of three categories: Some see their work as a career, others see it as just a job, and still others see it as a calling.[2] It's this third category of people, perhaps unsurprisingly, who exhibit higher performance and a greater sense of satisfaction with their jobs. The key for you is to determine what you care about *now*—what drives you, what you're passionate about, what truly motivates you—and build from there. It's quite possible that what drove your career in your twenties is no longer appealing. Don't force your 40-, 50-, or 60-year-old self into your 20-year-old sense of ambition. Even if you don't find your true calling, you will at least increase the odds of finding a meaningful work experience.

See if parts of your job are "craftable"

There has been considerable research on the idea of job crafting, in which you tweak certain aspects of your job to gain a greater sense of meaning and satisfaction. Research by Wrzesniewski and two other organizational behavior scholars, Justin Berg and Jane Dutton, has shown that people can be quite imaginative and effective at reimagining the design of their job in personally meaningful ways.

For example, if you enjoy analysis but not sales, can you adjust your responsibilities in that direction? If you love interacting with others but feel lonely, can you find ways to partner more on projects? One participant from Berg, Dutton, and Wrzesniewski's research redesigned her marketing job to include

more event planning, even though it wasn't originally part of her job. The reason was quite simple:
She liked it and was good at it, and by doing so, she
could add value to the company and to her own work
experience.[3]

Or consider this activity: Imagine that you're a job
architect, and do a "before" and "after" sketch of your
job responsibilities, with the "before" representing
the uninspiring status quo and the "after" representing future possibilities.[4] What novel tweaks can you
make to redesign your job, even slightly? Sometimes
even the smallest adjustments can lead to qualita-
tively meaningful changes in your work experience.

Ignite your passion outside of work

It might be a latent hobby you've told yourself you
don't have the time for, a personal project that isn't
related to your job or career, or a "side hustle" where

you can experiment with innovative or entrepreneurial ideas on a smaller scale. Having an outlet for your passion outside of work can counterbalance the monotony of the nine-to-five daily grind. These inspirational endeavors can even have unintended positive spillover effects at work, giving you energy and inspiration to craft your job or reengage with parts of it you actually like.[5]

If all else fails, make a change

Think about changing your career like you'd think about changing your house. When you originally bought your house, you had certain requirements. But since then, your priorities may have changed, or maybe you have simply outgrown it. Do you move, renovate, or stay put? You can think the exact same way about your job and career. Have your priorities and needs changed? Can you tweak or "renovate" your job? Or do you need to move on?

Of course, if you choose to change your career, you'll want to think it through and prepare yourself before jumping in with both feet. Network with people in professions you might be interested in, get your finances in order, and test out the new career (perhaps on the weekend or at night) before making the change. It can feel daunting to change everything so suddenly, but it's important to consider the option if you're truly feeling a deep sense of malaise at work.

The most important thing, though, if you're finding your interest waning at work, is not to lose hope. You *can* find ways to ignite your passion again—or at least make slight changes so you won't feel so hopeless. You'll likely be surprised at how resilient and resourceful you are as you walk down the path of career renovation.

ANDY MOLINSKY is a professor of organizational behavior at the Brandeis International Business School. He's the author of *Global Dexterity*: *How to Adapt Your Behavior Across Cultures Without Losing Yourself in the Process* (Harvard Business Review Press, 2013) and *Reach: A New Strategy to Help You*

Step Outside Your Comfort Zone, Rise to the Challenge, and Build Confidence (Avery, 2017).

Notes

1. E. O'Boyle and A. Mann, "American Workplace Changing at a Dizzying Pace," Gallup News, February 15, 2017.
2. K. Brooks, "Job, Career, Calling: Key to Happiness and Meaning at Work?" *Psychology Today*, June 29, 2012, https://www.psychologytoday.com/blog/career-transitions/201206/job-career-calling-key-happiness-and-meaning-work.
3. J. M. Berg, J. E. Dutton, and A. Wrzesniewski, "What Is Job Crafting and Why Does It Matter?" working paper, Center for Positive Organizational Scholarship, Ross School of Business, University of Michigan, 2007.
4. L. Lee, "Should Employees Design Their Own Jobs?" *Insights by Stanford Business*, January 22, 2016.
5. "The Positive Effect of Creative Hobbies on Performance at Work," *PsyBlog* (blog), April 28, 2014, http://www.spring.org.uk/2014/04/the-positive-effect-of-creative-hobbies-on-performance-at-work.php.

Reprinted from hbr.org, originally published
July 10, 2017 (product #H03RL0).

3

You Don't Find Your Purpose— You Build It

By John Coleman

H ow do I find my purpose?"

Ever since Daniel Gulati, Oliver Segovia, and I published our book *Passion and Purpose* six years ago, I've received hundreds of questions—from younger and older people alike—about purpose. We're all looking for purpose. Most of us feel that we've never found it, we've lost it, or in some way we're falling short.

But in the midst of all this angst, I think we're also suffering from what I see as fundamental misconceptions about purpose, neatly encapsulated by the question I receive most frequently: *How do I find my purpose?* Challenging these misconceptions can help us all develop a more well-rounded vision of purpose.

Misconception #1: Purpose is only a thing you find

On social media, I often see an inspiring quotation attributed to Mark Twain: "The two most important days in your life are the day you are born and the day you find out why." It neatly articulates what I'll call the "Hollywood version" of purpose. Like Neo in *The Matrix* or Rey in *Star Wars*, we're all just moving through life waiting until fate delivers a higher calling to us.

Make no mistake: That can happen, at least in some form. I recently saw Scott Harrison, founder and CEO of respected nonprofit Charity: Water, speak, and in many ways his story was about how he found a higher purpose after a period of wandering. But I think it's more rare than most people think. For the average 20-year-old in college or 40-year-old in an unfulfilling job, searching for the silver bullet to give life meaning is more likely to end in frustration than fulfillment.

In achieving professional purpose, most of us have to focus as much on *making* our work meaningful as in *taking* meaning from it. Put differently, purpose is a thing you build, not a thing you find. Almost any work can possess remarkable purpose. School bus drivers bear enormous responsibility—caring for and keeping safe dozens of children—and are an essential part of assuring our children receive the education they need and deserve. Nurses play an essential role not simply in treating people's medical conditions but also in guiding them through some of life's most difficult times. Cashiers can be a friendly, uplifting interaction in someone's day—often desperately needed—or a forgettable or regrettable one. But in each of these instances, purpose is often primarily derived from focusing on what's so meaningful and purposeful about the job and on doing it in such a way that that meaning is enhanced and takes center stage. Sure, some jobs more naturally lend themselves to a sense of meaning, but many require at least some deliberate effort to invest them with the purpose we seek.

Misconception #2:
Purpose is a single thing

The second misconception I often hear is that purpose can be articulated as a single thing. Some people genuinely do seem to have an overwhelming purpose in their lives. Mother Teresa lived her life to serve the poor. Samuel Johnson poured every part of himself into his writing. Marie Curie devoted her energy to her work.

And yet even these luminaries had other sources of purpose in their lives. Mother Teresa served the poor as part of what she believed was a higher calling. Curie, the Nobel prize–winning scientist, was also a devoted wife and mother (she wrote a biography of her husband, Pierre, and one of her daughters— Irene—won her own Nobel prize). And Johnson, beyond his writing, was known to be a great humanitarian in his community, often caring personally for the poor.

Most of us will have multiple sources of purpose in our lives. I find purpose in my children, my marriage, my faith, my writing, my work, and my community. For almost everyone, there's no one thing we can find. It's not *purpose* but *purposes* we are looking for: the multiple sources of meaning that help us find value in our work and lives. Professional commitments are only one component of this meaning, and often our work isn't central to our purpose but a conduit to helping others, including our families and communities. Acknowledging that there are multiple sources of purpose takes the pressure off of finding one single thing to give our lives meaning.

Misconception #3:
Purpose is stable over time

It's common now for people to have multiple careers in their lifetimes. I know one individual, for example, who recently left a successful private equity career to found a startup. I know two more who recently left business careers to run for elective office. And whether or not we switch professional commitments, most of us will experience personal phases in which our sources of meaning change—childhood, young adulthood, parenthood, and empty-nesting, to name a few.

This evolution in our sources of purpose isn't flaky or demonstrative of a lack of commitment but rather natural and good. Just as we all find meaning in multiple places, the sources of that meaning can and do change over time. My focus and sense of purpose at 20 was dramatically different in many ways than it is now, and the same could be said of almost anyone you meet.

How do you find your purpose? That's the wrong question to ask. We should be looking to endow everything we do with purpose, to allow for the multiple sources of meaning that will naturally develop in our lives, and to be comfortable with those sources changing over time. Unpacking what we mean by "purpose" can allow us to better understand its presence and role in our lives.

JOHN COLEMAN is a coauthor of the book *Passion and Purpose: Stories from the Best and Brightest Young Business Leaders* (Harvard Business Review Press, 2013).

Reprinted from hbr.org, originally published
October 20, 2012 (product #H03YZX).

4

How to Find Meaning in a Job That Isn't Your True Calling

By Emily Esfahani Smith

hy do so few people find fulfillment in their work?

A few years ago I posed this question to Amy Wrzesniewski, a Yale School of Management professor who studies these issues, and she offered an explanation that made a lot of sense. Students, she told me, "think their calling is under a rock, and if they turn over enough rocks, they will find it."

Surveys confirm that meaning is the top thing millennials say they want from a job. And yet her research shows that less than 50% of people see their work as a calling. So many of her students are left feeling anxious and frustrated and completely unsatisfied by the good jobs and careers they do secure.[1]

What they—and many of us, I think—fail to realize is that work can be meaningful even if you don't think of it as a calling. The four most common occupations in America are retail salesperson, cashier, food preparer or server, and office clerk—jobs that aren't typically associated with meaning.[2] But all have something in common with roles that are considered meaningful, such as clergy, teachers, and doctors: They exist to help others. And as Adam Grant, an organizational psychologist and professor at the University of Pennsylvania's Wharton School, has shown, people who see their work as a form of giving consistently rank their jobs as more meaningful.[3]

That means you can find meaning in nearly any role in nearly any organization. After all, most companies create products or services to fill a need in the world, and all employees contribute in their own way. The key is to become more conscious about the service you're providing—as a whole and personally.

How? One way is to connect with the end user or beneficiary. In one study, Grant and his colleagues found that fundraisers in a university call center who'd been introduced to a student whose education was being paid for by the money raised spent 142% more time on the phone with potential donors and raised 171% more cash than peers who hadn't met those scholarship recipients. Whether your customers are external or internal, an increased focus on them, and how you help them live their lives or do their jobs, can help you find more meaning in yours.

Another strategy is to constantly remind yourself of your organization's overarching goal. There's a great story about a janitor that John F. Kennedy ran into at NASA in 1962. When the president asked him what he was doing, the man said, "I'm helping put a man on the moon." Life is Good is an apparel company best known for colorful T-shirts with stick-figure designs, but its mission is to spread optimism and hope throughout the world, and that's something that even the company's warehouse employees understand. If you work for an accounting firm, you're helping people or companies with the unpleasant task of doing their taxes. If you're a fast-food cook, you're providing a family with a cheap and delicious meal. Each of these jobs serves a purpose in the world.

Even if you can't get excited about your company's mission or customers, you can still adopt a service mindset by thinking about how your work helps those you love. Consider a study of women working in a coupon-processing factory in Mexico. Researchers led by Jochen Menges, a professor of leadership and organizational behavior at WHU–Otto Beisheim School of Management, found that those who described the work as dull were generally less productive than those who said it was rewarding. But the effects went away for those in the former group who saw the work (however tedious) as a way to support their families. With that attitude, they were just as productive and energized as the coupon processors who didn't mind the task. Many people understand the purpose of their jobs in a similar manner. The work they do helps them pay their mortgage, go on vacation—or even support a hobby that gives meaning to their lives, like volunteer tutoring, gardening, or woodworking.

Not everyone finds their one true calling. But that doesn't mean we're doomed to work meaningless jobs. If we reframe our tasks as opportunities to help others, any occupation can feel more significant.

EMILY ESFAHANI SMITH is the author of *The Power of Meaning: Crafting a Life That Matters* (Crown, 2017) and an editor at Stanford University's Hoover Institution, where she manages the Ben Franklin Circles project, a collaboration with the 92nd Street Y and Citizen University to build meaning in local communities.

Notes

1. E. Esfahani Smith and J. L. Aaker, "Millennial Searchers," *New York Times*, November 30, 2013; and A. Wrzesniewski et al., "Jobs, Careers, and Callings: People's

Relations to Their Work," *Journal of Research in Personality* 31 (1997).

2. Bureau of Labor Statistics, U.S. Department of Labor, "Retail Salespersons and Cashiers Were Occupations with Highest Employment in May 2015," *The Economics Daily*, November 2017.

3. A. Grant, "In the Company of Givers and Takers," *Harvard Business Review*, April 2013.

Reprinted from hbr.org, originally published
August 3, 2012 (product #H03T83).

5

You're Never Done Finding Purpose at Work

By Dan Pontefract

D o you dread going into the office on Monday morning? Maybe a new boss has entered the equation, creating a rift between how you once felt and how you feel now. Perhaps your company has recently been acquired, and the culture has changed. Maybe you simply have outgrown your role and are bored to tears in your cubicle.

I have found that whether or not we enjoy our work often boils down to how our job fits with our sense of purpose. Where we work, the role we hold, our broader sense of purpose—all three are subject to change. Thus, if we want to stay in the "sweet spot" among these three, we must not fear career transitions or even change itself; indeed, we must seek them out.

Having a sense of purpose in our life is critical to well-being. In fact, in a longitudinal study, researchers found that people who demonstrate a sense of purpose in their lives have a 15% lower risk of early death.[1] Having a sense of purpose in our roles at work is equally important. And yet it's not enough to find that sense of purpose once—you have to continually find it as circumstances (and you) change.

"I am cautious and alert and mindful that the battle is not won yet" is how Céline Schillinger, an executive at vaccine maker Sanofi Pasteur, describes staying on this learning journey. "I will not fall into complacency. No matter what, I will continue to hone myself." In 2001 Schillinger landed a position in France at the company. To date, she has occupied positions in human resources, product development, and stakeholder engagement. She moved to Boston in 2015 to focus on quality innovation. "I would define myself as a person under construction," she told me. "I'm always trying to enrich my experience by adding bits and pieces wherever I go. I experiment in my roles and push for uncomfortableness to eventually gain new knowledge out of each situation."

Schillinger's story shows that you don't have to quit your company to stay engaged. However, sometimes a more radical change is needed. Consider the story of Mana Ionescu. She worked hard to climb the ladder at the U.S.-based company she worked for, and she was in line for the director role. But Ionescu was frustrated by the transactional nature of her work. Creativity was minimal. Inspiration was nominal. "There must be more to my working life than just sitting here making money and not actually making an impact," she thought. She decided to leave her organization and founded Lightspan Digital, a digital marketing company based in Chicago that specializes in social media, email, and content marketing. Ionescu recognized that she had to take charge of both her personal life and her working life—and ever since, she has been living *and* working with a sense of purpose. It's up to each of us to know when to make that leap.

Try this exercise. At the end of the workday, jot down approximately how much time you spent in each of the following three mindsets:

- *Job mindset.* When someone has a job mindset, they resort to a "paycheck mentality," performing their duties in return for compensation and not much else.

- *Career mindset.* This mindset occurs when an individual is focused on increasing or advancing their salary, title, power, team size, or sphere of control.

- *Purpose mindset.* Feeling passionate, innovative, and committed are hallmarks of this mindset, as is having an outward-looking focus on serving the broader organization or key stakeholders. Here, your professional purpose feels aligned with your personal purpose.

Keep a log for a couple of weeks, and see whether you fall into one of these mindsets more than the others. If the job and career mindsets total more than 50% of your time, that may be a warning sign that you need to restate or redefine your personal purpose.

No one lives in the purpose mindset all the time, but spending too much time in the career or job mindsets is destructive: You are certain to be dissatisfied with your job, and these mindsets can end up harming your reputation, chances of promotion, and long-term prospects. While everyone should be trying to develop and grow, focusing too much on your career or your paycheck can lead to bad behaviors such as bullying and selfishness or simply trying to exert too much control over others. Before that happens, seek a new role, and perhaps a new organization, that rebalances your equation.

If you have never created a personal declaration of purpose, now is the time. A declaration of purpose is a simple statement about how you will decide to live each and every day. Make it succinct, specific, jargon free, and expressive. Your statement ought to be personal, and it should integrate your strengths, interests, and core ambitions. Here's mine: "We're not here to see through each other; we're here to see each other through." (For more on a personal declaration of purpose, see chapter 6 of this book.)

Take into account all three types of purpose: personal, job, and organization. But don't shortchange your personal purpose, which is a common error, according to A. R. Elangovan, a professor of organizational behavior at the University of Victoria in Canada. As he told me, "Especially in contrast to organizational and role purpose, where multiple stakeholders shape the outcomes, my advice is to invest as much effort [as possible] into figuring out our personal purpose."

Life is short. You deserve to work in a role, and for an organization, where your personal purpose shines. But you cannot leave it up to the organization, your boss, or your team. It really does come down to you defining and enacting your purpose.

DAN PONTEFRACT is the author of *The Purpose Effect: Building Meaning in Yourself, Your Role, and Your Organization* (2016) and *Flat Army: Creating a Connected and Engaged Organization* (Wiley, 2013). He is chief envisioner at wireless and internet services company TELUS.

Note

1. P. L. Hill and N. A. Turiano, "Purpose in Life as a Predictor of Mortality Across Adulthood," *Psychological Science* 25, no. 7 (2014).

Reprinted from hbr.org, originally published May 20, 2016 (product #H02WJI).

6

From Purpose
to Impact

By Nick Craig and Scott A. Snook

The two most important days in
your life are the day you are born
and the day you find out why.

—Mark Twain

Over the past five years, there's been an explosion of interest in purpose-driven leadership. Academics argue persuasively that an executive's most important role is to be a steward of the organization's purpose. Business experts make the case that purpose is a key to exceptional performance, while psychologists describe it as the pathway to greater well-being.

Doctors have even found that people with purpose in their lives are less prone to disease. Purpose is increasingly being touted as the key to navigating the complex, volatile, ambiguous world we face today, where strategy is ever changing and few decisions are obviously right or wrong.

Despite this growing understanding, however, a big challenge remains. In our work training thousands of managers at organizations from GE to the Girl Scouts, and teaching an equal number of executives and students at Harvard Business School, we've found that fewer than 20% of leaders have a strong sense of their own individual purpose. Even fewer can distill their purpose into a concrete statement. They may be able to clearly articulate their organization's mission: Think of Google's "To organize the world's information and make it universally accessible and useful," or Charles Schwab's "A relentless ally for the individual investor." But when asked to describe their own purpose, they typically fall back on something generic and nebulous: "Help others excel." "Ensure success." "Empower my people." Just as problematic, hardly any of them have a clear plan for translating purpose into action. As a result, they limit their aspirations and often fail to achieve their most ambitious professional and personal goals.

Our purpose is to change that—to help executives find and define their leadership purpose and put it to use. Building on the seminal work of our colleague Bill George, our programs initially covered a wide range of topics related to authentic leadership, but in recent years purpose has emerged as the cornerstone of our teaching and coaching. Executives tell us it is the key to accelerating their growth and deepening their impact, in both their professional and personal lives. Indeed, we believe that the process of articulating your purpose and finding the courage to live it— what we call *purpose to impact*—is the single most important developmental task you can undertake as a leader.

Consider Dolf van den Brink, the president and CEO of Heineken USA. Working with us, he identified a decidedly unique purpose statement—"To be the wuxia master who saves the kingdom"—which reflects his love of Chinese kung fu movies, the inspiration he takes from the wise, skillful warriors in them, and the realization that he, too, revels in high-risk situations that compel him to take action. With that impetus, he was able to create a plan for reviving a challenged legacy business during extremely difficult economic conditions. We've also watched a retail operations chief call on his newly clarified purpose—"Compelled to make things better, whomever, wherever, however"—to make the "hard, cage-rattling changes" needed to beat back a global competitor. And we've seen a factory director in Egypt use his purpose—"Create families that excel"—to persuade employees that they should honor the 2012 protest movement not by joining the marches but by maintaining their loyalties to one another and keeping their shared operation running.

We've seen similar results outside the corporate world. Kathi Snook (Scott's wife) is a retired army colonel who'd been struggling to reengage in work after several years as a stay-at-home mom. But after nailing her purpose statement—"To be the gentle, behind-the-scenes, kick-in-the-ass reason for success," something she'd done throughout her military career and with her kids—she decided to run for a hotly contested school committee seat, and won.

And we've implemented this thinking across organizations. Unilever is a company that is committed to purpose-driven leadership, and Jonathan Donner, the head of global learning there, has been a key partner in refining our approach. Working with his company and several other organizations, we've helped more than 1,000 leaders through the purpose-to-impact process and have begun to track and review their progress over the past two to three years. Many have seen dramatic results, ranging from two-step promotions to sustained improvement in business results. Most important, the vast majority tell us

57

they've developed a new ability to thrive in even the most challenging times.

In this article, we share our step-by-step framework to start you down the same path. We'll explain how to identify your purpose and then develop an impact plan to achieve concrete results.

What is purpose?

Most of us go to our graves with our music still inside us, unplayed.

—Oliver Wendell Holmes

Your leadership purpose is who you are and what makes you distinctive. Whether you're an entrepreneur at a startup or the CEO of a *Fortune* 500 company, a call center rep or a software developer, your purpose is your brand, what you're driven to achieve, the magic that makes you tick. It's not *what* you do, it's *how* you do your job and *why*—the strengths and passions you bring to the table no matter where you're seated. Although you may express your purpose in different ways in different contexts, it's what everyone close to you recognizes as uniquely you and would miss most if you were gone.

When Kathi Snook shared her purpose statement with her family and friends, the response was instantaneous and overwhelming: "Yes! That's you—all business, all the time!" In every role and every context—as captain of the army gymnastics team, as a math teacher at West Point, informally with her family and friends—she had always led from behind, a gentle but forceful catalyst for others' success. Through this new lens, she was able to see herself—and her future—more clearly. When Dolf van den Brink revealed his newly articulated purpose to his wife, she easily recognized the "wuxia master" who had led his employees through the turmoil of serious fighting and unrest in the Congo and was now ready to attack the challenges at Heineken USA head-on.

At its core, your leadership purpose springs from your identity, the essence of who you are. Purpose is not a list of the education, experience, and skills you've gathered in your life. We'll use ourselves as examples. The fact that Scott is a retired army colonel with an MBA and a PhD is not his purpose. His purpose is "to help others live more 'meaning-full' lives." Purpose is also not a professional title, limited to your current job or organization. Nick's purpose is not "To lead the Authentic Leadership Institute." That's his job. His purpose is "To wake you up and have you find that you are home." He has been doing just that since he was a teenager, and if you sit next to him on the shuttle from Boston to New York, he'll wake you up (figuratively), too. He simply can't help himself.

Purpose is definitely not some jargon-filled catch-all ("Empower my team to achieve exceptional business results while delighting our customers"). It should be specific and personal, resonating with you and you alone. It doesn't have to be aspirational or cause based ("Save the whales" or "Feed the hungry"). And it's not what you think it should be—it's who you can't help being. In fact, it might not necessarily be all that flattering ("Be the thorn in people's side that keeps them moving!").

How do you find it?

To be nobody but yourself in a world
which is doing its best, night and day,
to make you everybody else, means to
fight the hardest battle which any human
being can fight; and never stop fighting.

—E.E. Cummings

Finding your leadership purpose is not easy. If it were, we'd all know exactly why we're here and be living that purpose every minute of every day. As E.E. Cummings suggests, we are constantly bombarded by powerful messages (from parents, bosses, management gurus, advertisers, celebrities) about what we should be (smarter, stronger, richer) and about how to lead (empower others, lead from behind, be authentic, distribute power). To figure out who you are in such a world, let alone "be nobody but yourself," is indeed hard work. However, our experience shows that when you have a clear sense of who you are, everything else follows naturally.

Some people will come to the purpose-to-impact journey with a natural bent toward introspection and reflection. Others will find the experience uncomfortable and anxiety provoking. A few will just roll their eyes. We've worked with leaders of all stripes and can attest that even the most skeptical discover personal and professional value in the experience. At one multinational corporation, we worked with a senior lawyer who characterized himself as "the least likely person to ever find this stuff useful." Yet he became such a supporter that he required all his people to do the program. "I have never read a self-help book, and I don't plan to," he told his staff. "But if you want to become an exceptional leader, you have to know your leadership purpose." The key to engaging both the dreamers and the skeptics is to build a process that has room to express individuality but also offers step-by-step practical guidance.

The first task is to mine your life story for common threads and major themes. The point is to identify your core, lifelong strengths, values, and passions— those pursuits that energize you and bring you joy. We use a variety of prompts but have found three to be most effective:

- What did you especially love doing when you were a child, before the world told you what you should or shouldn't like or do? Describe a moment and how it made you feel.

- Tell us about two of your most challenging life experiences. How have they shaped you?

- What do you enjoy doing in your life now that helps you sing your song?

We strongly recommend grappling with these questions in a small group of a few peers, because we've found that it's almost impossible for people to identify their leadership purpose by themselves. You can't get a clear picture of yourself without trusted colleagues or friends to act as mirrors.

After this reflective work, take a shot at crafting a clear, concise, and declarative statement of purpose: "My leadership purpose is _____." The words in your purpose statement must be yours. They must capture your essence. And they must call you to action.

To give you an idea of how the process works, consider the experiences of a few executives. When we asked one manager about her childhood passions, she told us about growing up in rural Scotland and delighting in "discovery" missions. One day, she and a friend set out determined to find frogs and spent the whole day going from pond to pond, turning over every stone. Just before dark, she discovered a single frog and was triumphant. The purpose statement she later crafted—"Always find the frogs!"—is perfect for her current role as the senior VP of R&D for her company.

Another executive used two "crucible" life experiences to craft her purpose. The first was personal: Years before, as a divorced young mother of two, she found herself homeless and begging on the street, but she used her wits to get back on her feet. The second was professional: During the economic crisis of 2008, she had to oversee her company's retrenchment from Asia and was tasked with closing the flagship operation in the region. Despite the near hopeless job environment, she was able to help every one of her employees find another job before letting them go. After discussing these stories with her group, she shifted her purpose statement from "Continually and consistently develop and facilitate the growth and development of myself and others leading to great performance" to "With tenacity, create brilliance."

Dolf came to his "wuxia master" statement after exploring not only his film preferences but also his extraordinary crucible experience in the Congo, when militants were threatening the brewery he managed and he had to order it barricaded to protect his employees and prevent looting. The Egyptian factory director focused on family as his purpose because his stories revealed that familial love and support had been the key to facing every challenge in his life, while the retail operations chief used "Compelled to improve" after realizing that his greatest achievements had always come when he pushed himself and others out of their comfort zones.

As you review your stories, you will see a unifying thread, just as these executives did. Pull it, and you'll uncover your purpose. (The exhibit "Purpose Statements" offers a sampling of purpose statements.)

Purpose statements

FROM BAD . . .	TO GOOD . . .
Lead new markets department to achieve exceptional business results	Eliminate chaos
Be a driver in the infrastructure business that allows each person to achieve their needed outcomes while also mastering the new drivers of our business as I balance my family and work demands	Bring water and power to the two billion people who do not have it
Continually and consistently develop and facilitate the growth and development of myself and others, leading to great performance	With tenacity, create brilliance

How do you put your purpose into action?

*This is the true joy in life, the being
used for a purpose recognized by
yourself as a mighty one.*

—George Bernard Shaw

Clarifying your purpose as a leader is critical, but writing the statement is not enough. You must also envision the impact you'll have on your world as a result of living your purpose. Your actions—not your words—are what really matter. Of course, it's virtually impossible for any of us to fully live into our purpose 100% of the time. But with work and careful planning, we can do it more often, more consciously, wholeheartedly, and effectively.

Purpose-to-impact plans differ from traditional development plans in several important ways: They start with a statement of leadership purpose rather than of a business or career goal. They take a holistic view of professional and personal life rather than ignore the fact that you have a family or outside interests and commitments. They incorporate meaningful, purpose-infused language to create a document that speaks to you, not just to any person in your job or role. They force you to envision long-term opportunities for living your purpose (three to five years out) and then help you to work backward from there (two years out, one year, six months, three months, 30 days) to set specific goals for achieving them.

When executives approach development in this purpose-driven way, their aspirations—for instance, Kathi's decision to get involved in the school board, or the Egyptian factory director's ambition to run manufacturing and logistics across the Middle East— are stoked. Leaders also become more energized in their current roles. Dolf's impact plan inspired him to tackle his role at Heineken USA with four mottos

Purpose-to-impact planning versus traditional development planning

PURPOSE-TO-IMPACT PLANNING	TRADITIONAL DEVELOPMENT PLANNING
Uses meaningful, purpose-infused language	Uses standard business language
Is focused on strengths to realize career aspirations	Is focused on weaknesses to address performance
Elicits a statement of leadership purpose that explains how you will lead	States a business- or career-driven goal
Sets incremental goals related to living your leadership purpose	Measures success using metrics tied to the firm's mission and goals
Focuses on the future, working backward	Focuses on the present, working forward
Is unique to you; addresses who you are as a leader	Is generic; addresses the job or role
Takes a holistic view of work and family	Ignores goals and responsibilities outside the office

for his team: "Be brave," "Decide and do," "Hunt as a pack," and "Take it personally." When Unilever executive Jostein Solheim created a development plan around his purpose—"To be part of a global movement that makes changing the world seem fun and achievable"—he realized he wanted to stay on as CEO of the Ben & Jerry's business rather than moving up the corporate ladder.

Let's now look at a hypothetical purpose-to-impact plan (representing a composite of several people with whom we've worked) for an in-depth view of the process. "Richard" arrived at his purpose only after being prodded into talking about his lifelong passion for sailing; suddenly, he'd found a set of experiences and language that could redefine how he saw his job in procurement.

Richard's development plan leads with the *purpose statement* he crafted: "To harness all the elements to win the race." This is followed by *an explanation* of why that's his purpose: Research shows

71

that understanding what motivates us dramatically increases our ability to achieve big goals.

Next, Richard addresses his *three- to five-year goals* using the language of his purpose statement. We find that this is a good time frame to target first; several years is long enough that even the most disillusioned managers could imagine they'd actually be living into their purpose by then. But it's not so distant that it creates complacency. A goal might be to land a top job—in Richard's case, a global procurement role—but the focus should be on how you will do it, what kind of leader you'll be.

Then he considers *two-year goals*. This is a time frame in which the grand future and current reality begin to merge. What new responsibilities will you take on? What do you have to do to set yourself up for the longer term? Remember to address your personal life, too, because you should be more fully living into your purpose everywhere. Richard's goals explicitly reference his family, or "shore team."

A PURPOSE-TO-IMPACT PLAN

This sample plan shows how "Richard" uses his unique leadership purpose to envision big-picture aspirations and then work backward to set more-specific goals.

1. Create purpose statement

To harness all the elements to win the race

2. Write explanation

I love to sail. In my teens and twenties, I raced high-performance three-man skiffs and almost made it to the Olympics. Now sailing is my hobby and passion—a challenge that requires discipline, balance, and coordination. You never know what the wind will do next, and in the end, you win the race only by relying on your team's combined capabilities, intuition, and flow. It's all about how you read the elements.

(Continued)

A PURPOSE-TO-IMPACT PLAN

3. Set three- to five-year goals

Be known for training the best crews and winning the big races: Take on a global procurement role, and use the opportunity to push my organization ahead of competitors

How will I do it?

- Make everyone feel they're part of the same team
- Navigate unpredictable conditions by seeing wind shears before everyone else
- Keep calm when we lose individual races; learn and prepare for the next ones

Celebrate my shore team: Make sure the family has one thing we do that binds us

4. Set two-year goals

Win the gold: Implement a new procurement model, redefining our relationship with suppliers and generating 10% cost savings for the company

Tackle next-level racing challenge: Move into a European role with broader responsibilities

How will I do it?

- Anticipate and then face the tough challenges
- Insist on innovative yet rigorous and pragmatic solutions
- Assemble and train the winning crew

Develop my shore team: Teach the boys to sail

(Continued)

A PURPOSE-TO-IMPACT PLAN

5. Set one-year goals

Target the gold: Begin to develop new procurement process

Win the short race: Deliver Sympix project ahead of expectations

Build a seaworthy boat: Keep TFLS process within cost and cash forecast

How will I do it?

- Accelerate team reconfiguration
- Get buy-in from management for new procurement approach

Invest in my shore team: Take a two-week vacation, no email

6. Map out critical next steps

Assemble the crew: Finalize key hires

Chart the course: Lay the groundwork for Sympix and TFLS projects

How will I do it?

Six months:

- Finalize succession plans
- Set out Sympix timeline

Three months:

- Land a world-class replacement for Jim
- Schedule "action windows" to focus with no email

30 days:

- Bring Alex in Shanghai on board
- Agree on TFLS metrics
- Conduct one-day Sympix off-site

(Continued)

A PURPOSE-TO-IMPACT PLAN

Reconnect with my shore team: Be more present with Jill and the boys

7. Examine key relationships

Sarah, HR manager

Jill, manager of my shore team

The fifth step—setting *one-year goals*—is often the most challenging. Many people ask, "What if most of what I am doing today isn't aligned in any way with my leadership purpose? How do I get from here to there?" We've found two ways to address this problem. First, think about whether you can rewrite the narrative on parts of your work, or change the way you do some tasks, so that they become an expression of your purpose. For example, the phrase "seaworthy boat" helps Richard see the meaning in managing a basic procurement process. Second, consider whether you can add an activity that is 100% aligned with your purpose. We've found that most people can manage to devote 5% to 10% of their time to something that energizes them and helps others see their strengths. Take Richard's decision to contribute to the global strategic procurement effort: It's not part of his "day job," but it gets him involved in a more purpose-driven project.

Now we get to the nitty-gritty. What are the *critical next steps* that you must take in the coming six months, three months, and 30 days to accomplish the one-year goals you've set out? The importance of small wins is well documented in almost every management discipline from change initiatives to innovation. In detailing your next steps, don't write down all the requirements of your job. List the activities or results that are most critical given your newly clarified leadership purpose and ambitions. You'll probably notice that a number of your tasks seem much less urgent than they did before, while others you had pushed to the side take priority.

Finally, we look at the *key relationships* needed to turn your plan into reality. Identify two or three people who can help you live more fully into your leadership purpose. For Richard, it is Sarah, the HR manager who will help him assemble his crew, and his wife, Jill, the manager of his "shore team."

Executives tell us that their individual purpose-to-impact plans help them stay true to their short- and long-term goals, inspiring courage, commitment, and focus. When they're frustrated or flagging, they pull out the plans to remind themselves what they want to accomplish and how they'll succeed. After creating his plan, the retail operations chief facing global competition said he's no longer "shying away from things that are too hard." Dolf van den Brink said: "I'm much clearer on where I really can contribute and where not. I have full clarity on the kind of roles

I aspire to and can make explicit choices along the way." What creates the greatest leaders and companies? Each of them operates from a slightly different set of assumptions about the world, their industry, what can or can't be done. That individual perspective allows them to create great value and have significant impact. They all operate with a unique leadership purpose. To be a truly effective leader, you must do the same. Clarify your purpose, and put it to work.

NICK CRAIG is the president of the Authentic Leadership Institute. **SCOTT A. SNOOK** is currently an associate professor of organizational behavior at Harvard Business School. He served in the U.S. Army Corps of Engineers for over 22 years.

Reprinted from *Harvard Business Review*,
May 2014 (product #R1405H).

7

Five Questions to Help Your Employees Find Their Inner Purpose

By Kristi Hedges

ow can leaders help employees find meaning at work?

Organizations spend considerable resources on corporate values and mission statements, but even the most inspiring of these—from Volvo's commitment to safety to Facebook's desire to connect people—tend to fade into the background during the daily bustle of the workday.

What workers really need to feel engaged in and satisfied by their jobs is an inner sense of purpose. As Deloitte found in a 2016 study, people feel loyal to companies that support their own career and life ambitions—in other words, what's meaningful to them.[1]

And, although that research focused on millennials, in the decade I've spent coaching seasoned executives, I've found that it's a common attitude across generations. No matter one's level, industry, or career, we all need to find a personal sense of meaning in what we do.

Leaders can foster this inner sense of purpose—what matters right now, in each individual's life and career—with simple conversation. One technique is action identification theory, which posits that there are many levels of description for any action.[2] For example, right now I'm writing this article. At a low level, I'm typing words on a keyboard. At a high level, I'm creating better leaders. When leaders walk employees up this ladder, they can help them find meaning in even the most mundane tasks.

Regular check-ins that use five areas of inquiry are another way to help employees explore and call out their inner purpose. Leaders can ask:

What are you good at doing? Which work activities require less effort for you? What do you take on because you believe you're the best person to do it? What have you gotten noticed for throughout your career? The idea here is to help people identify their strengths and open possibilities from there.

What do you enjoy? In a typical workweek, what do you look forward to doing? What do you see on your calendar that energizes you? If you could design your job with no restrictions, how would you spend your time? These questions help people find or rediscover what they love about work.

What feels most useful? Which work outcomes make you most proud? Which of your tasks are most critical to the team or organization? What are the highest priorities for your life and how does your work fit in? This line of inquiry high-lights the inherent value of certain work.

What creates a sense of forward momentum? What are you learning that you'll use in the future? What do you envision for yourself next? How is your work today getting you closer to what you want for yourself? The goal here is to show how today's work helps the individual advance toward future goals.

How do you relate to others? Which working partnerships are best for you? What would an office of your favorite people look like? How does your work enhance your family and social connections? These questions encourage people to think about and foster relationships that make work more meaningful.

It's not easy to guide others toward purpose, but these strategies can help.

KRISTI HEDGES is a senior leadership coach who specializes in executive communications and the author of *The Inspiration Code: How the Best Leaders Energize People Every Day* (AMACOM, 2017) and *The Power of Presence: Unlock Your Potential to Influence and Engage Others* (AMACOM, 2011). She is the president of the Hedges Company and a faculty member at Georgetown University's Institute for Transformational Leadership.

Notes

1. Deloitte, "2016 Deloitte Millennial Survey: Winning Over the Next Generation of Leaders," 2016, https://www2.deloitte.com/content/dam/Deloitte/global/Documents/About-Deloitte/gx-millenial-survey-2016-exec-summary.pdf.
2. R. R. Vallacher and D. M. Wegner, *A Theory of Action Identification* (Hillsdale, NJ: Lawrence Erlbaum Associates, 1985).

Reprinted from hbr.org, originally published August 17, 2017 (product #H03U96).

8

How to Make Work More Meaningful for Your Team

By Lewis Garrad and Tomas Chamorro-Premuzic

There is a well-known story about a janitor at NASA who, when asked by John F. Kennedy what his job was, responded, "I'm helping to put a man on the moon." This anecdote is often used to show how even the most mundane job can be seen as meaningful with the right mindset and under good leadership.

Today, more and more employees demand much more than a good salary from their jobs. Money may lure people into particular positions, but purpose, meaning, and the prospect of interesting and valuable work determines both their tenure and how hard they will work while they are on the job. Finding meaning at work has become so important that there are even public rankings for the most meaningful jobs.[1] Although there are many factors that determining how appealing a position tends to be, those that contribute to improving other people's lives (such as those in health care and social work) are ranked at the top. Interestingly, meta-analytic studies indicate that there is only a marginal association between pay and job satisfaction.[2] By that reasoning, a lawyer who earns $150,000 a year is no more engaged than a freelance designer who earns $35,000 a year.

Research consistently shows that people who experience meaningful work report better health, more well-being, and a clearer sense of teamwork and engagement. They bounce back faster from setbacks and are more likely to view mistakes as learning opportunities rather than failures. In other words, people at work who experience their job as meaningful are more likely to thrive and grow. This is why businesses with a stronger and clearer sense of purpose tend to perform better financially. Unsurprisingly, the most successful companies in the world are also the best places in the world to work.[3]

Over the past few decades, a great deal of research has shown that leaders play a significant role in helping employees understand why their roles matter. Furthermore, the leadership characteristics that enable these cultures of meaning and purpose to engage employees are a reflection of a leader's personality—which has been proven to have a strong impact on team and organizational performance.[4]

In particular, research suggests that there are four key personality characteristics that determine leaders' ability to make other people's jobs more meaningful, namely:

> *They are curious and inquisitive.* Studies show that people tend to experience work as meaningful when they feel like they are contributing to creating something new—especially when

they feel able to explore, connect and have an impact.[5] Curious leaders help people find meaning at work by exploring, asking questions, and engaging people in ideas about the future. In a way, curious leaders help employees find something meaningful by providing a wider range of possibilities for how work gets done, as opposed to being very prescriptive and micromanaging people. Curious leaders also detest monotony and are more likely to get bored, so they will always be looking for people to come up with new ideas to make their own experience of work more interesting.

They are challenging and relentless. One of the greatest problems organizations must solve is the inertia and stagnation that follow, or even anticipate, success. Research shows that optimistic people who expect to do well don't try as hard as people who expect to struggle or

fail.[6] Leaders who remain ambitious in the face
of both failure and success, and who push their
people to remain dissatisfied with their accom-
plishments, instill a deeper sense of purpose
in their teams and organizations. As a result
employees feel a sense of progress, reinvention,
and growth, which in turn results in a more
meaningful and positive work experience.

They hire for values and culture fit. Research
shows that people only find something valuable
if it aligns with their core needs and motives.
This is why the fit between an individual's
personal values and the culture of the organization they work in is such an important driver
of their performance. In fact, you are better off
not hiring the "best" people but instead looking
for those who are a good fit for your organization. Values function like an inner compass or
lens through which we assign meaning to the

world. Leaders who pay attention to what *each* individual values are more likely to hire people who will find it easier to connect with their colleagues and the wider organization, all of which help to drive a sense of meaning.[7]

They are able to trust people. Most individuals hate being micromanaged. Overpowering and controlling bosses are a serious source of disempowerment for employees. They drain the value from the work they do and make employees feel worthless. In stark contrast, leaders who know how to trust people are more likely to give them room to experiment and grow. In particular, they help their employees mold their roles—something researchers call "job crafting." Employees who customize their job tend to feel a much greater sense of importance and value because they feel that their manager actually trusts them.

Note that all of the above four qualities ought to exist in concert. A boss who is relentless but not trusting might seek to "keep people on their toes" by being erratic or unpredictable—a sure way to hurt performance and morale. A boss who is challenging but not curious may come across as a bully, while a boss who's trusting but not challenging will seem like a pushover. In short, there is a clear difference between making work meaningful and making it fun or easy, just like there is a big difference between an engaged and a happy employee. Whereas engagement results in enthusiasm, drive, and motivation—all of which increase performance and are therefore valuable to the organization—happiness can lead to complacency. To be a good leader, focus on helping employees find meaning in their achievements, rather than just enjoy their time at the office.

LEWIS GARRAD is a senior consultant and advisor at Mercer | Sirota. TOMAS CHAMORRO-PREMUZIC is the CEO of Hogan

Assessments, a professor of business psychology at University College London and at Columbia University, and an associate at Harvard's Entrepreneurial Finance Lab. His latest book is *The Talent Delusion: Why Data, Not Intuition, Is the Key to Unlocking Human Potential* (2017).

Notes

1. "The Most and Least Meaningful Jobs," Payscale, http://www.payscale.com/data-packages/most-and-least-meaningful-jobs/least-meaningful-jobs.
2. T. A. Judge et al., "The Relationship Between Pay and Job Satisfaction: A Meta-Analysis of the Literature," *Journal of Vocational Behavior* 77, no. 2 (2010).
3. M. F. Steger, "Measuring Meaningful Work: The Work and Meaning Inventory (WAMI)," *Journal of Career Assessment* 20, no. 3 (2012); G. Spreitzer et al., "A Socially Embedded Model of Thriving at Work," *Organization Science* 16, no. 5 (2005); and C. M. Gartenberg et al., "Corporate Purpose and Financial Performance," Columbia Business School Research Paper no. 16–69, June 30, 2016.
4. M. Carton, "'I'm Not Mopping the Floors, I'm Putting a Man on the Moon': How NASA Leaders Enhanced the Meaningfulness of Work by Changing the Meaning of Work," *Administrative Science Quarterly*, 2017; and C. A. O'Reilly et al., "The Promise and Problems of

Organizational Culture," *Group and Organization Management* 39, no. 6 (2014).

5. A. Wrzesniewski and J. E. Dutton, "Crafting a Job: Revisioning Employees as Active Crafters of Their Work," *Academy of Management Review* 26, no. 2 (2001).

6. H. B. Kappes and G. Oettingen, "Positive Fantasies About Idealized Futures Sap Energy," *Journal of Experimental Social Psychology* 47, no. 4 (2011).

7. T. Schnell et al., "Predicting Meaning in Work: Theory, Data, Implications," *Journal of Positive Psychology* 8, no. 6 (2013); A. L. Kristof-Brown et al., "Consequences of Individuals' Fit at Work: A Meta-Analysis of Person-Job, Person-Organization, Person-Group, and Person-Supervisor Fit," *Personnel Psychology* 58 (2005); and A. Bhaduri, *Don't Hire the Best: An Essential Guide to Building the Right Team* (Hogan Press, 2013).

Reprinted from hbr.org, originally published
August 9, 2017 (product #H03U4D).

9

The Power of
Small Wins

By Teresa M. Amabile and Steven J. Kramer

W hat is the best way to drive innovative work inside organizations? Important clues hide in the stories of world-renowned creators. It turns out that ordinary scientists, marketers, programmers, and other unsung knowledge workers, whose jobs require creative productivity every day, have more in common with famous innovators than most managers realize. The workday events that ignite their emotions, fuel their motivation, and trigger their perceptions are fundamentally the same.

The Double Helix, James Watson's 1968 memoir about discovering the structure of DNA, describes the roller coaster of emotions he and Francis Crick experienced through the progress and setbacks of the work that eventually earned them the Nobel Prize. After the excitement of their first attempt to build a DNA model, Watson and Crick noticed some serious flaws. According to Watson, "Our first minutes with the models . . . were not joyous." Later that evening, "a shape began to emerge which brought back our spirits." But when they showed their "breakthrough" to colleagues, they found that their model would not work. Dark days of doubt and ebbing motivation followed. When the duo finally had their bona fide breakthrough, and their colleagues found no fault with it, Watson wrote, "My morale skyrocketed, for I suspected that we now had the answer to the riddle." Watson and Crick were so driven by this success that they practically lived in the lab, trying to complete the work.

Throughout these episodes, Watson and Crick's progress—or lack thereof—ruled their reactions. In our recent research on creative work inside businesses, we stumbled upon a remarkably similar phenomenon. Through exhaustive analysis of diaries kept by knowledge workers, we discovered the "progress principle": Of all the things that can boost emotions, motivation, and perceptions during a workday, the single most important is making progress in meaningful work. And the more frequently people experience that sense of progress, the more likely they are to be creatively productive in the long run. Whether they are trying to solve a major scientific mystery or simply produce a high-quality product or service, everyday progress—even a small win—can make all the difference in how they feel and perform.

The power of progress is fundamental to human nature, but few managers understand it or know how to leverage progress to boost motivation. In fact, work motivation has been a subject of long-standing debate. In a survey asking about the keys to motivating workers, we found that some managers ranked recognition for good work as most important, while others put more stock in tangible incentives. Some focused on the value of interpersonal support, while still others thought clear goals were the answer. Interestingly, very few of our surveyed managers ranked progress first. (See the sidebar "A Surprise for Managers.")

If you are a manager, the progress principle holds clear implications for where to focus your efforts. It suggests that you have more influence than you may realize over employees' well-being, motivation, and creative output. Knowing what serves to catalyze and nourish progress—and what does the opposite— turns out to be the key to effectively managing people and their work.

In this article, we share what we have learned about the power of progress and how managers can leverage it. We spell out how a focus on progress translates into concrete managerial actions and provide a checklist to help make such behaviors habitual. But to clarify why those actions are so potent, we first

A SURPRISE FOR MANAGERS

In a 1968 issue of HBR, Frederick Herzberg published a now-classic article titled "One More Time: How Do You Motivate Employees?" Our findings are consistent with his message: People are most satisfied with their jobs (and therefore most motivated) when those jobs give them the opportunity to experience achievement. The diary research we describe in this article—in which we microscopically examined the events of thousands of workdays, in real time—uncovered the mechanism underlying the sense of achievement: making consistent, meaningful progress.

But managers seem not to have taken Herzberg's lesson to heart. To assess contemporary awareness of the importance of daily work progress, we recently administered a survey to 669 managers of varying levels from dozens of companies around the world. We asked about the managerial tools that can affect employees'

(Continued)

A SURPRISE FOR MANAGERS

motivation and emotions. The respondents ranked five tools—support for making progress in the work, recognition for good work, incentives, interpersonal support, and clear goals—in order of importance.

Of the managers who took our survey, 95% would probably be surprised to learn that supporting progress is the primary way to elevate motivation—because that's the percentage who failed to rank progress number one. In fact, only 35 managers ranked progress as the number one motivator—a mere 5%. The vast majority of respondents ranked support for making progress dead last as a motivator and third as an influence on emotion. They ranked "recognition for good work (either public or private)" as the most important factor in motivating workers and making them happy. In our diary study, recognition certainly did boost inner work life. But it wasn't nearly as prominent as progress. Besides, without work achievements, there is little to recognize.

describe our research and what the knowledge workers' diaries revealed about their "inner work lives."

Inner work life and performance

For nearly 15 years, we have been studying the psychological experiences and the performance of people doing complex work inside organizations. Early on, we realized that a central driver of creative, productive performance was the quality of a person's inner work life: the mix of emotions, motivations, and perceptions over the course of a workday. How happy workers feel; how motivated they are by an intrinsic interest in the work; how positively they view their organization, their management, their team, their work, and themselves—all these combine either to push them to higher levels of achievement or to drag them down.

To understand such interior dynamics better, we asked members of project teams to respond individually to an end-of-day email survey during the course of the project—just over four months, on average. (For more on this research, see our article "Inner Work Life: Understanding the Subtext of Business Performance," HBR, May 2007.) The projects—inventing kitchen gadgets, managing product lines of cleaning tools, and solving complex IT problems for a hotel empire, for example—all involved creativity. The daily survey inquired about participants' emotions and moods, motivation levels, and perceptions of the work environment that day, as well as what work they did and what events stood out in their minds.

Twenty-six project teams from seven companies participated, comprising 238 individuals. This yielded nearly 12,000 diary entries. Naturally, every individual in our population experienced ups and downs. Our goal was to discover the states of inner work life and the workday events that correlated with the highest levels of creative output.

In a dramatic rebuttal to the commonplace claim that high pressure and fear spur achievement, we found that, at least in the realm of knowledge work, people are more creative and productive when their inner work lives are positive—when they feel happy, are intrinsically motivated by the work itself, and have positive perceptions of their colleagues and the organization. Moreover, in those positive states, people are more committed to the work and more collegial toward those around them. Inner work life, we saw, can fluctuate from one day to the next—sometimes wildly—and performance along with it. A person's inner work life on a given day fuels his or her performance for the day and can even affect performance the *next* day.

Once this "inner work-life effect" became clear, our inquiry turned to whether and how managerial action could set it in motion. What events could evoke positive or negative emotions, motivations, and perceptions? The answers were tucked within our research participants' diary entries. There are predictable triggers that inflate or deflate inner work life, and, even accounting for variation among individuals, they are pretty much the same for everyone.

The power of progress

Our hunt for inner work-life triggers led us to the progress principle. When we compared our research participants' best and worst days (based on their overall mood, specific emotions, and motivation levels), we found that the most common event triggering a "best day" was any progress in the work by the individual or the team. The most common event triggering a "worst day" was a setback.

Consider, for example, how progress relates to one component of inner work life: overall mood ratings. Steps forward occurred on 76% of people's best-mood days. By contrast, setbacks occurred on only 13% of those days. (See the figure "What happens on good days and bad days?")

Two other types of inner work-life triggers also occur frequently on best days: *catalysts*, actions that directly support work, including help from a person or group, and *nourishers*, events such as shows of respect and words of encouragement. Each has an opposite: *inhibitors*, actions that fail to support or actively hinder work, and *toxins*, discouraging or undermining events. Whereas catalysts and inhibitors are directed at the project, nourishers and toxins are directed at the person. Like setbacks, inhibitors and toxins are rare on days of great inner work life.

Events on worst-mood days are nearly the mirror image of those on best-mood days. Here, setbacks predominated, occurring on 67% of those days; progress occurred on only 25% of them. Inhibitors and toxins also marked many worst-mood days, and catalysts and nourishers were rare.

This is the progress principle made visible: If a person is motivated and happy at the end of a workday, it's a good bet that he or she made some progress.

If the person drags out of the office disengaged and joyless, a setback is most likely to blame.

When we analyzed all 12,000 daily surveys filled out by our participants, we discovered that progress and setbacks influence all three aspects of inner work life. On days when they made progress, our participants reported more positive *emotions*. They not only were in a more upbeat mood in general but also expressed more joy, warmth, and pride. When they suffered setbacks, they experienced more frustration, fear, and sadness.

Motivations were also affected: On progress days, people were more intrinsically motivated—by interest in and enjoyment of the work itself. On setback days, they were not only less intrinsically motivated but also less extrinsically motivated by recognition. Apparently, setbacks can lead a person to feel generally apathetic and disinclined to do the work at all.

Perceptions differed in many ways, too. On progress days, people perceived significantly more positive

What happens on good days and bad days?

Progress—even a small step forward—occurs on many of the days people report being in a good mood. Events on bad days—setbacks and other hindrances—are nearly the mirror image of those on good days.

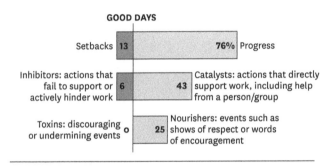

GOOD DAYS

Setbacks **13** — **76%** Progress

Inhibitors: actions that fail to support or actively hinder work **6** — **43** Catalysts: actions that directly support work, including help from a person/group

Toxins: discouraging or undermining events **o** — **25** Nourishers: events such as shows of respect or words of encouragement

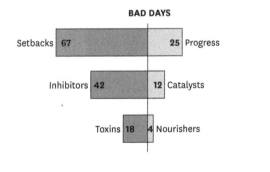

BAD DAYS

Setbacks **67** — **25** Progress

Inhibitors **42** — **12** Catalysts

Toxins **18** — **4** Nourishers

challenge in their work. They saw their teams as more mutually supportive and reported more positive interactions between the teams and their supervisors. On a number of dimensions, perceptions suffered when people encountered setbacks. They found less positive challenge in the work, felt that they had less freedom in carrying it out, and reported that they had insufficient resources. On setback days, participants perceived both their teams and their supervisors as less supportive.

To be sure, our analyses establish correlations but do not prove causality. Were these changes in inner work life the result of progress and setbacks, or was the effect the other way around? The numbers alone cannot answer that. However, we do know, from reading thousands of diary entries, that more-positive perceptions, a sense of accomplishment, satisfaction, happiness, and even elation often followed progress. Here's a typical post-progress entry, from a programmer: "I smashed that bug that's been frustrating me for almost a calendar week. That may not be an event to you, but I live a very drab life, so I'm all hyped."

Likewise, we saw that deteriorating perceptions, frustration, sadness, and even disgust often followed setbacks. As another participant, a product marketer, wrote, "We spent a lot of time updating the cost reduction project list, and after tallying all the numbers, we are still coming up short of our goal. It is discouraging to not be able to hit it after all the time spent and hard work."

Almost certainly, the causality goes both ways, and managers can use this feedback loop between progress and inner work life to support both.

Minor milestones

When we think about progress, we often imagine how good it feels to achieve a long-term goal or experience a major breakthrough. These big wins are great—but they are relatively rare. The good news is that even small wins can boost inner work life tremendously. Many of the progress events our research participants reported represented only minor steps forward. Yet they often evoked outsize positive reactions. Consider this diary entry from a programmer in a high-tech company, which was accompanied by very positive self-ratings of her emotions, motivations, and perceptions that day: "I figured out why something was not working correctly. I felt relieved and happy because this was a minor milestone for me."

Even ordinary, incremental progress can increase people's engagement in the work and their happiness during the workday. Across all the types of events our participants reported, a notable proportion (28%) that had a minor impact on the project had a major impact on people's feelings about it. Because inner work life has such a potent effect on creativity and productivity, and because small but consistent steps forward shared by many people can accumulate into excellent execution, progress events that often go unnoticed are critical to the overall performance of organizations.

Unfortunately, there is a flip side. Small losses or setbacks can have an extremely negative effect on inner work life. In fact, our study and research by others show that negative events can have a more powerful impact than positive ones. Consequently, it is especially important for managers to minimize daily hassles. (See again the figure "What happens on good days and bad days?")

Progress in meaningful work

We've shown how gratifying it is for workers when they are able to chip away at a goal, but recall what we said earlier: The key to motivating performance is supporting progress in *meaningful* work. Making headway boosts your inner work life, but only if the work matters to you.

Think of the most boring job you've ever had. Many people nominate their first job as a teenager— washing pots and pans in a restaurant kitchen, for example, or checking coats at a museum. In jobs like those, the power of progress seems elusive. No matter how hard you work, there are always more pots to wash and coats to check; only punching the time clock at the end of the day or getting the paycheck at the end of the week yields a sense of accomplishment.

In jobs with much more challenge and room for creativity, like the ones our research participants had, simply "making progress"—getting tasks done— doesn't guarantee a good inner work life, either. You may have experienced this rude fact in your own job, on days (or in projects) when you felt demotivated, devalued, and frustrated, even though you worked hard and got things done. The likely cause is your perception of the completed tasks as peripheral or irrelevant. For the progress principle to operate, the work must be meaningful to the person doing it.

In 1983, Steve Jobs was trying to entice John Sculley to leave a wildly successful career at PepsiCo to become Apple's new CEO. Jobs reportedly asked him, "Do you want to spend the rest of your life selling sugared water or do you want a chance to change the world?" In making his pitch, Jobs leveraged a potent psychological force: the deep-seated human desire to do meaningful work.

Fortunately, to feel meaningful, work doesn't have to involve putting the first personal computers in the hands of ordinary people, or alleviating poverty, or helping to cure cancer. Work with less profound importance to society can matter if it contributes value to something or someone important to the worker. Meaning can be as simple as making a useful and high-quality product for a customer or providing a genuine service for a community. It can be supporting a colleague or boosting an organization's profits by reducing inefficiencies in a production process. Whether the goals are lofty or modest, as long as they are meaningful to the worker and it is clear how his or her efforts contribute to them, progress toward them can galvanize inner work life.

In principle, managers shouldn't have to go to extraordinary lengths to infuse jobs with meaning. Most jobs in modern organizations are potentially meaningful for the people doing them. However, managers can make sure that employees know just how their work is contributing. And, most important, they can avoid actions that negate its value. (See the sidebar "How Work Gets Stripped of Its Meaning.") All the participants in our research were doing work that should have been meaningful; no one was washing pots or checking coats. Shockingly often, however, we saw potentially important, challenging work losing its power to inspire.

HOW WORK GETS STRIPPED OF ITS MEANING

Diary entries from 238 knowledge workers who were members of creative project teams revealed four primary ways in which managers unwittingly drain work of its meaning.

Managers may dismiss the importance of employees' work or ideas. Consider the case of Richard, a senior lab technician at a chemical company, who found meaning in helping his new-product development team solve complex technical problems. However, in team meetings over the course of a three-week period, Richard perceived that his team leader was ignoring his suggestions and those of his teammates. As a result, he felt that his contributions were not meaningful, and his spirits flagged. When at last he believed that he was again making a substantive contribution to the success of the project, his mood

(Continued)

HOW WORK GETS STRIPPED OF ITS MEANING

improved dramatically: "I felt much better at today's team meeting. I felt that my opinions and information were important to the project and that we have made some progress."

They may destroy employees' sense of ownership of their work. Frequent and abrupt reassignments often have this effect. This happened repeatedly to the members of a product development team in a giant consumer products company, as described by team member Bruce: "As I've been handing over some projects, I do realize that I don't like to give them up. Especially when you have been with them from the start and are nearly to the end. You lose ownership. This happens to us way too often."

Managers may send the message that the work employees are doing will never see the light of day. They can signal this—unintentionally—by shifting their priorities or changing their minds about how something should be done. We saw the latter in an internet technology company after user-interface developer Burt had spent weeks designing seamless transitions for non-English-speaking users. Not surprisingly, Burt's mood was seriously marred on the day he reported this incident: "Other options for the international [interfaces] were [given] to the team during a team meeting, which could render the work I am doing useless."

They may neglect to inform employees about unexpected changes in a customer's priorities. Often, this arises from poor customer management or inadequate communication within the company. For example, Stuart, a data transformation expert at an IT company, reported deep frustration and low

(Continued)

HOW WORK GETS STRIPPED OF ITS MEANING

motivation on the day he learned that weeks of the team's hard work might have been for naught: "Found out that there is a strong possibility that the project may not be going forward, due to a shift in the client's agenda. Therefore, there is a strong possibility that all the time and effort put into the project was a waste of our time."

Supporting progress: catalysts and nourishers

What can managers do to ensure that people are motivated, committed, and happy? How can they support workers' daily progress? They can use catalysts and nourishers, the other kinds of frequent "best day" events we discovered.

Catalysts are actions that support work. They include setting clear goals, allowing autonomy, providing sufficient resources and time, helping with the work, openly learning from problems and successes, and allowing a free exchange of ideas. Their opposites, inhibitors, include failing to provide support and actively interfering with the work. Because of their impact on progress, catalysts and inhibitors ultimately affect inner work life. But they also have a more immediate impact: When people realize that they have clear and meaningful goals, sufficient resources, helpful colleagues, and so on, they get an instant boost to their emotions, their motivation to do a great job, and their perceptions of the work and the organization.

Nourishers are acts of interpersonal support, such as respect and recognition, encouragement, emotional comfort, and opportunities for affiliation. Toxins, their opposites, include disrespect, discouragement, disregard for emotions, and interpersonal conflict. For good and for ill, nourishers and toxins affect inner work life directly and immediately.

Catalysts and nourishers—and their opposites—can alter the meaningfulness of work by shifting people's perceptions of their jobs and even themselves. For instance, when a manager makes sure that people have the resources they need, it signals to them that what they are doing is important and valuable. When managers recognize people for the work they do, it signals that they are important to the organization. In this way, catalysts and nourishers can lend greater meaning to the work—and amplify the operation of the progress principle.

The managerial actions that constitute catalysts and nourishers are not particularly mysterious; they may sound like Management 101, if not just common sense and common decency. But our diary study reminded us how often they are ignored or forgotten. Even some of the more attentive managers in the companies we studied did not consistently provide catalysts and nourishers. For example, a supply chain specialist named Michael was, in many ways and on most days, an excellent subteam manager. But he was occasionally so overwhelmed that he became toxic toward his people. When a supplier failed to complete a "hot" order on time and Michael's team had to resort to air shipping to meet the customer's deadline, he realized that the profit margin on the sale would be blown. In irritation, he lashed out at his subordinates, demeaning the solid work they had done and disregarding their own frustration with the supplier. In his diary, he admitted as much: "As of Friday, we have spent $28,000 in air freight to send 1,500 $30 spray jet mops to our number two customer. Another 2,800 remain on this order, and there is a good probability that they too will gain wings. I have turned from the kindly supply chain manager into the black-masked executioner. All similarity to civility is gone, our backs are against the wall, flight is not possible, therefore fight is probable."

Even when managers don't have their backs against the wall, developing long-term strategy and launching new initiatives can often seem more important—and perhaps sexier—than making sure subordinates have what they need to make steady progress and feel supported as human beings. But as we saw repeatedly in our research, even the best strategy will fail if managers ignore the people working in the trenches to execute it.

A model manager—and a tool for emulating him

We could explain the many (and largely unsurprising) moves that can catalyze progress and nourish spirits, but it may be more useful to give an example of a manager who consistently used those moves—and then to provide a simple tool that can help any manager do so.

Our model manager is Graham, whom we observed leading a small team of chemical engineers within a multinational European firm we'll call Kruger-Bern. The mission of the team's NewPoly project was clear and meaningful enough: Develop a safe, biodegradable polymer to replace petrochemicals in cosmetics and, eventually, in a wide range of consumer products. As in many large firms however, the project was nested in a confusing and sometimes threatening corporate setting of shifting top-management priorities, conflicting signals, and wavering commitments. Resources were uncomfortably tight, and uncertainty loomed over the project's future—and every team member's career. Even worse, an incident early in the project, in which an important customer reacted angrily to a sample, left the team reeling. Yet Graham was able to sustain team members' inner work lives by repeatedly and visibly removing obstacles, materially supporting progress, and emotionally supporting the team.

Graham's management approach excelled in four ways. First, he established a positive climate, one event at a time, which set behavioral norms for the entire team. When the customer complaint stopped the project in its tracks, for example, he engaged immediately with the team to analyze the problem, without recriminations, and develop a plan for repairing the relationship. In doing so, he modeled how to respond to crises in the work: not by panicking or pointing fingers but by identifying problems and their causes and developing a coordinated action plan. This is both a practical approach and a great way to give subordinates a sense of forward movement even in the face of the missteps and failures inherent in any complex project.

Second, Graham stayed attuned to his team's everyday activities and progress. In fact, the nonjudgmental climate he had established made this happen naturally. Team members updated him frequently—

without being asked—on their setbacks, progress, and plans. At one point, one of his hardest-working colleagues, Brady, had to abort a trial of a new material because he couldn't get the parameters right on the equipment. It was bad news, because the New-Poly team had access to the equipment only one day a week, but Brady immediately informed Graham. In his diary entry that evening, Brady noted, "He didn't like the lost week but seemed to understand." That understanding assured Graham's place in the stream of information that would allow him to give his people just what they needed to make progress.

Third, Graham targeted his support according to recent events in the team and the project. Each day, he could anticipate what type of intervention—a catalyst or the removal of an inhibitor; a nourisher or some antidote to a toxin—would have the most impact on team members' inner work lives and progress. And if he could not make that judgment, he asked. Most days it was not hard to figure out, as on the day he received some uplifting news about his bosses' commitment to the project. He knew the team was jittery about a rumored corporate reorganization and could use the encouragement. Even though the clarification came during a well-earned vacation day, he immediately got on the phone to relay the good news to the team.

Finally, Graham established himself as a resource for team members rather than a micromanager; he was sure to check in while never seeming to check *up* on them. Superficially, checking in and checking up seem quite similar, but micromanagers make four kinds of mistakes. First, they fail to allow autonomy in carrying out the work. Unlike Graham, who gave the NewPoly team a clear strategic goal but respected members' ideas about how to meet it, micromanagers dictate every move. Second, they frequently ask subordinates about their work without providing any real help. By contrast, when one of Graham's team members reported problems, Graham helped analyze them—remaining open to alternative interpretations—and often ended up helping to get things back on track. Third, micromanagers are quick to affix personal blame when problems arise, leading subordinates to hide problems rather than honestly discuss how to surmount them, as Graham did with Brady. And fourth, micromanagers tend to hoard information to use as a secret weapon. Few realize how damaging this is to inner work life. When subordinates perceive that a manager is withholding potentially useful information, they feel infantilized, their motivation wanes, and their work is handicapped. Graham was quick to communicate upper management's views of the project, customers' opinions and needs, and possible sources of assistance or resistance within and outside the organization.

In all those ways, Graham sustained his team's positive emotions, intrinsic motivation, and favorable perceptions. His actions serve as a powerful example of how managers at any level can approach each day determined to foster progress.

We know that many managers, however well-intentioned, will find it hard to establish the habits that seemed to come so naturally to Graham. Awareness, of course, is the first step. However, turning an awareness of the importance of inner work life into routine action takes discipline. With that in mind, we developed a checklist for managers to consult on a daily basis (see the sidebar "The Daily Progress Checklist"). The aim of the checklist is managing for meaningful progress, one day at a time.

The progress loop

Inner work life drives performance; in turn, good performance, which depends on consistent progress, enhances inner work life. We call this the "progress loop"—it reveals the potential for self-reinforcing benefits.

So, the most important implication of the progress principle is this: By supporting people and their daily progress in meaningful work, managers improve not only the inner work lives of their employees but also the organization's long-term performance, which enhances inner work life even more. Of course, there is a dark side—the possibility of negative feedback loops. If managers fail to support progress and the people trying to make it, inner work life suffers and so does performance; and degraded performance further undermines inner work life.

A second implication of the progress principle is that managers needn't fret about trying to read the psyches of their workers or manipulate complicated incentive schemes to ensure that employees are motivated and happy. As long as managers show basic respect and consideration, they can focus on supporting the work itself.

To become an effective manager, you must learn to set this positive feedback loop in motion. That may require a significant shift. Business schools, business books, and managers themselves usually focus on managing organizations or people. But if you focus on managing progress, the management of people—and even of entire organizations—becomes much more feasible. You won't have to figure out how to x-ray the inner work lives of subordinates; if you facilitate their steady progress in meaningful work, make that progress salient to them, and treat them well, they will experience the emotions, motivations, and perceptions necessary for great performance. Their superior work will contribute to organizational success. And here's the beauty of it: They will love their jobs.

TERESA M. AMABILE is the Edsel Bryant Ford Professor of Business Administration at Harvard Business School and the author of *Creativity in Context* (Westview Press, 1996). STEVEN J. KRAMER is an independent researcher, writer, and consultant. He is a coauthor of "Creativity Under the Gun" (HBR, August 2002) and "Inner Work Life" (HBR, May 2007). Amabile and Kramer are the coauthors of *The Progress*

Principle: Using Small Wins to Ignite Joy, Engagement, and Creativity at Work (Harvard Business Review Press, 2011).

Reprinted from *Harvard Business Review,*
May 2011 (product #R1105C).

THE DAILY PROGRESS CHECKLIST

Near the end of each workday, use this checklist to review the day and plan your managerial actions for the next day. After a few days, you will be able to identify issues by scanning the boldface words.

First, focus on progress and setbacks and think about specific events (catalysts, nourishers, inhibitors, and toxins) that contributed to them. Next, consider any clear inner-work-life clues and what further information they provide about progress and other events. Finally, prioritize for action.

The action plan for the next day is the most important part of your daily review: What is the one thing you can do to best facilitate progress?

(Continued)

141

THE DAILY PROGRESS CHECKLIST

Progress

Which 1 or 2 events today indicated either a small win or a possible breakthrough? (Describe briefly.)

_____

_____

Catalysts

- ☐ Did the team have clear short- and long-term **goals** for meaningful work?

- ☐ Did team members have sufficient **autonomy** to solve problems and take ownership of the project?

- ☐ Did they have all the **resources** they needed to move forward efficiently?

- ☐ Did they have sufficient **time** to focus on meaningful work?

- ☐ Did I discuss **lessons** from today's successes and problems with my team?

- ☐ Did I give or get them **help** when they needed or requested it? Did I encourage team members to help one another?

- ☐ Did I help **ideas** flow freely within the group?

Nourishers

- ☐ Did I show **respect** to team members by recognizing their contributions to progress, attending to their ideas, and treating them as trusted professionals?

- ☐ Did I **encourage** team members who faced difficult challenges?

- ☐ Did I **support** team members who had a personal or professional problem?

- ☐ Is there a sense of personal and professional **affiliation** and camaraderie within the team?

(Continued)

THE DAILY PROGRESS CHECKLIST

Setbacks

Which 1 or 2 events today indicated either a small setback or a possible crisis? (Describe briefly.)

_____

_____

Inhibitors

- ☐ Was there any confusion regarding long- or short-term **goals** for meaningful work?

- ☐ Were team members overly **constrained** in their ability to solve problems and feel ownership of the project?

- ☐ Did they lack any of the **resources** they needed to move forward effectively?

- ☐ Did they lack sufficient **time** to focus on meaningful work?

- ☐ Did I or others fail to provide needed or requested **help**?

☐ Did I "punish" failure or neglect to find **lessons** and/or opportunities in problems and successes?

☐ Did I or others cut off the presentation or debate of **ideas** prematurely?

Toxins

☐ Did I **disrespect** any team members by failing to recognize their contributions to progress, not attending to their ideas, or not treating them as trusted professionals?

☐ Did I **discourage** a member of the team in any way?

☐ Did I **neglect** a team member who had a personal or professional problem?

☐ Is there tension or **antagonism** among members of the team or between team members and me?

(Continued)

THE DAILY PROGRESS CHECKLIST

Inner work life

- Did I see any indications of the quality of my subordinates' inner work lives today? _____

  _____

  _____

- Perceptions of the work, team, management, firm _____

  _____

- Emotions _____

  _____

  _____

- Motivation _____

  _____

- What specific events might have affected inner work life today? _____

  _____

Action plan

- What can I do tomorrow to strengthen the catalysts and nourishers identified and provide the ones that are lacking? _____

_____

_____

_____

_____

- What can I do tomorrow to start eliminating the inhibitors and toxins identified? _____

_____

_____

_____

_____

_____

_____

10

The Founder of TOMS on Reimagining the Company's Mission

By Blake Mycoskie

I n the fall of 2012 I did something I never thought I'd do: I took a sabbatical from TOMS. It was not your typical travel-the-world sabbatical. My wife, Heather, and I moved to Austin, Texas, where I'd grown up, and I used the physical and psychological separation from the company to do some soul-searching.

In the six years since I'd founded TOMS, it had grown from a startup based in my Venice, California, apartment to a global company with more than $300 million in revenue. I still owned 100% of it, and we were still delivering on our promise to give a pair of shoes to someone in need for every pair sold, but

I felt disillusioned. My days were monotonous, and I had lost my connection to many of the executives who were running daily operations. What had once been my reason for being now felt like a job.

During my months away, I did a lot of thinking about my personal "why." I knew why I had started the company and why people joined me in the early days. And I still believed in our mission and the impact we were making. But I was no longer sure why I wanted—or even if I did want—to continue driving the business forward.

Eventually I came to a surprising conclusion: I felt lost because TOMS had become more focused on process than on purpose. We were concentrating so hard on the "what" and "how" of scaling up that we'd forgotten our overarching mission, which is to use business to improve lives. That is our greatest competitive advantage: It allows us to build an emotional bond with customers and motivate employees, because they know they are shopping and working for a movement bigger than themselves.

After my time away from the business, I returned with renewed energy. My mission was clear: Make TOMS a movement again.

The company's genesis

I got the idea for TOMS on something like a sabbatical. After founding and selling several companies (a door-to-door laundry business, an outdoor advertising company, an online driver's education service) and making a brief detour into reality TV (I competed on *The Amazing Race* with my sister and created an all-reality cable channel), I decided to take some time off in 2006 to learn to play polo in Argentina. I know that sounds like a strange mix of pursuits, but I've always been happiest chasing my latest interest.

While in Buenos Aires, I met a woman who worked for a nonprofit, delivering shoes to children in poor rural areas. She invited me to accompany her, and the experience was truly life changing. In every town we were greeted with cheers and tears. I met a pair of brothers, ages 10 and 12, who had been sharing a single pair of adult-size shoes. Because the local schools required footwear, they had to take turns going to class. Their mother wept when I handed her shoes that actually fit her boys' feet. I couldn't believe that such a simple act could have such an enormous impact on people's lives.

I decided to do something more. Rather than go home and ask my friends to donate their hand-me-downs or make financial contributions, I would start a for-profit company based on the buy-one, give-one idea. I named it Shoes for Tomorrow, later shortened to Tomorrow's Shoes, and finally to TOMS so that the name would fit on the little tag on our shoes. (To this day, some people are puzzled when they meet me, because they're expecting a guy named Tom.)

My polo instructor, Alejo, and I persuaded a local shoemaker to help us make a more fashionable version of the *alpargata*, a canvas shoe worn by Argentines for a century. To borrow a term from Eric Ries's *The Lean Startup*, our first shoes were a "minimum viable product." They had glue stains on them, were in Argentine rather than U.S. sizes, and didn't always fit the same from pair to pair. But they were just good enough to test the concept among my friends in Los Angeles. My goal was to sell 250 pairs so that I could give away 250 pairs in Argentina.

Back home, I hosted a dinner party for some women friends to get their advice. They loved the shoes and were even more excited when I shared my vision of helping children in need. They suggested a number of local boutiques that might serve as retail outlets, so I went to one of them, American Rag, and asked to speak with the shoe buyer. I knew my shoes couldn't compete on quality or price alone, so I told the buyer why I wanted to sell them and give them away. The store became our first retail account.

On a Saturday morning soon after that, I woke up to find my BlackBerry vibrating. At the time, the TOMS website was set to email my phone every time we made a sale. Usually it was just family and friends placing orders, and the occasional buzzing was a nice surprise. But on this day the phone kept buzzing . . . and buzzing . . . and buzzing. At brunch I started flipping through the *Los Angeles Times* and saw that what I'd expected would be a short piece by its fashion writer on TOMS had landed on the front page of the Calendar section. By the end of the day we had sold 2,200 pairs of shoes. This was incredible—but it was also the company's first supply-chain management challenge. We had fewer than 200 pairs in my apartment.

Over the next six months I worked with a team of interns to turn my "shoe project" into a real company. We received a flood of additional press from *Vogue*, *People*, *Time*, *Elle*. Soon celebrities such as Tobey Maguire, Keira Knightley, and Scarlett Johansson were being photographed wearing TOMS. Nordstrom insisted on carrying our shoes. By the end of the summer we had sold 10,000 pairs. The "why" of TOMS was clearly resonating.

Disillusionment

By 2011 TOMS had an annual growth rate (for five years running) of 300%, and we'd recently given away our 10 millionth pair of shoes. The one-for-one model—initially dismissed by traditional businesspeople as nice but not financially sustainable—was clearly a success, and we'd decided to extend it to eyewear, giving away pairs of glasses or medical treatments to restore sight for pairs sold. We had set ourselves apart in other ways, too: A third of our revenue was coming from direct-to-consumer sales via our website, and we spent virtually nothing on traditional advertising, relying instead on our 5 million social media followers to create word-of-mouth buzz.

In September 2012 Heather and I got married. I'd brought in an experienced team of executives to manage the day-to-day operations, and for the first time since founding the business, I felt I could take a break from it. I was relieved but also deeply unsettled. The excitement and camaraderie of our startup was beginning to be replaced by a more hierarchical culture. The leadership team was bogged down in personality conflicts and bickering, with key members insisting that we implement processes and systems similar to those used at their previous companies. As an organization, we were so focused on protecting what we'd already built that no one was thinking about new possibilities. I noticed that longtime employees were starting to leave for more-entrepreneurial organizations, and I realized that, secretly, I wanted to follow them.

I'd started and sold companies before—but TOMS was different. It was more than a company to me: It was my life. So this period of uncertainty felt like having problems in a marriage. You thought you'd found your business soul mate, but you're not in love anymore. What do you do? For me, the sabbatical was like going into couples counseling. I wasn't walking away; I was putting in the work to see if TOMS and I could reconcile. If it had been a pure business problem, I would have organized a strategic offsite. But this was both corporate and personal. I needed to figure out the future course of the company and my role in it. And I tend to do my best thinking alone.

When I left for Austin, I was careful not to make a big deal of it—I told people the break was an extended honeymoon with Heather. But once there, I dedicated a lot of time to private contemplation. I also started talking to anyone I thought might offer good advice and inspire me. I spoke regularly with my executive coach, entrepreneur friends, and business and nonprofit leaders I admire. I traveled to conferences around the country to learn from experts in social enterprise and international development.

It was during this time that I read Simon Sinek's fantastic book *Start with Why*, which looks at leaders who inspire action, such as Martin Luther King Jr., and companies, such as Apple, that create products so compelling that fans will line up to buy them. Sinek argues that one can build and sustain these movements only when leading with the "why." People follow you, buy from you, when they believe what you believe.

The more I thought about this idea, the more I realized that TOMS had veered away from its "why." In the early days we always led with our story: We weren't selling shoes; we were selling the promise that each purchase would directly and tangibly benefit a child who needed shoes. But our desire to sustain the company's hypergrowth had pushed us away from that mission and into competing on the "what" and "how," just as every other shoe company does. In an effort to meet aggressive sales goals, we had begun promoting deals and discounts on our website—something we'd never done before. Our marketing increasingly felt product focused rather than purpose focused. And as the leader of TOMS, I was ultimately accountable for those mistakes. That was a tough pill to swallow.

Another breakthrough came during a Dallas Cowboys game. I was introduced to a man named Joe Ford, who told me that his son, Scott, was also using business to improve lives, but through the coffee trade in Rwanda. Joe explained the importance of water in the coffee supply chain. When beans are processed with clean as opposed to dirty water, they are transformed from a commodity to a specialty and can be sold at dramatically higher prices. Scott's company, Westrock Coffee, was helping Rwandan growers build community-owned washing stations to increase the value of their product and to prevent the spread of waterborne disease. It was also buying direct from growers, helping to break up unfair industry price controls, and offering low-interest loans as an alternative to those from predatory lenders. Best of all, Westrock was a profitable business that sold fantastic coffee.

After meeting Scott, I realized that a TOMS coffee venture could have a real impact—and maybe lift me out of the funk I was in. Like most entrepreneurs, I get a high from starting things and doing the unexpected. No one doubted our shoe business anymore, but few people would imagine that we could also sell coffee. And the expansion could pave the way for a new TOMS retail experience, something I had long wanted to try. We could create cafés and use them as community gathering places to share ideas, get inspired, and connect guests with the "why" of TOMS. The vision—and the challenge—pumped new life into me.

I told our senior executives about my idea. Like TOMS Shoes, TOMS Roasting would have a one-for-one model: For every bag of coffee we sold, we would provide a week's worth of water to a person in need. When they gave me the green light, I quickly assembled a small team of TOMS employees to get the project (code-named "Burlap") off the ground. I was still living in Austin, but the more I discussed my plans with Heather (an early TOMS employee who knew the business—and me—better than most people), the more she realized it was time for my sabbatical to end. We'd just bought a house, and we had a great group of friends, but in early 2013 she said to me, "Blake, we need to move back to L.A." If I was going to fully recommit to TOMS, it couldn't happen from afar.

The reentry

Coming back was great, but I quickly made some of the classic mistakes that founders do upon rejoining their companies. First, when I outlined my vision for using the coffee business to reinspire the "why" of TOMS, I did so without a fully thought-out plan. That made some of my coworkers anxious. Second, I asked the company's CMO to step down so that I could take over brand marketing and communications, which I considered to be key pieces of our new direction—not only for integrating the new business but also for reigniting the passion of our customers. But I quickly realized that I'm better in the founder's role—setting the vision and traveling the country to communicate it, not running marketing or any other department.

Despite these hiccups, by the end of 2013 we had launched the coffee business nationally in Whole Foods stores, opened up three of our own cafés, and started exploring international expansion. To date we have provided more than 175,000 weeks of clean drinking water to people in need around the world. The new product generated a ton of PR and got our customers excited about TOMS again. But most important, I believe, it gave our employees permission to think bigger, to challenge the status quo, and to reconnect with the mission of the business.

It also got me thinking bigger. I realized that my ultimate aim was to create the most influential, inspirational company in the world, which would be possible only with more help. I decided to meet with private equity firms that had a track record of helping entrepreneurial companies into the next stage of growth, and after a thorough search, I sold 50% of TOMS to Bain Capital in mid-2014. We clearly defined my role and responsibilities and agreed to hire a world-class CEO.

The man we found, Jim Alling, embodies the core values of TOMS. Although he scratched his head a bit over the "coffee decision" (he spent much of his career in senior roles at Starbucks), he understood what the move represented. Creating TOMS Roasting wasn't an attempt to compete with big chains but, rather, a bold move to reengage with the community and help more people. Over the past year Jim has brought great stability and strategic thinking to the business. We now also sell handbags to fund safe births for mothers and babies in need and backpacks to support anti-bullying programs.

As TOMS approaches its 10th anniversary, I feel more energized and committed than ever. As far as we've come, I still see tremendous opportunities to grow our movement. The "why" of TOMS—using business to improve lives—is bigger than myself, the shoes we sell, or any future products we might launch. It took going on a sabbatical to realize the power of what we've created—and the best way for me to move it forward. Now that I have a clear purpose and amazing partners supporting me, I'm ready for the company's next 10 years and the many adventures ahead.

BLAKE MYCOSKIE is the founder and chief shoe giver of TOMS.

Reprinted from *Harvard Business Review*,
January–February 2016 (product #R1601A).

Index

How to be human at work.

HBR's Emotional Intelligence Series features smart, essential reading on the human side of professional life from the pages of *Harvard Business Review*. Each book in the series offers uplifting stories, practical advice, and research from leading experts on how to tend to our emotional well-being at work.

Harvard Business Review Emotional Intelligence Series

Available in paperback or ebook format. The specially priced six-volume set includes:

- Mindfulness
- Resilience
- Influence and Persuasion
- Authentic Leadership
- Happiness
- Empathy